contents

cupcakes	2
cookies	30
glossary	60
conversion chart	62
index	63

NZ, Canada, US and UK readers
Please note that Australian cup and
spoon measurements are metric.
A conversion chart appears on page 62.

chocolate and coconut sponge cakes

4 eggs
¾ cup (165g) caster sugar
⅔ cup (100g)
   self-raising flour
⅓ cup (35g) cocoa powder
90g butter, melted
1 tablespoon hot water
⅔ cup (160ml)
   thickened cream
2 tablespoons
   caster sugar, extra
⅓ cup (15g) flaked coconut
chocolate ganache
200g dark eating chocolate,
   chopped coarsely
⅔ cup (160ml)
   thickened cream

1 Preheat oven to 180°C/160°C fan-forced. Grease two 9-hole friand pans.

2 Beat eggs in small bowl with electric mixer about 8 minutes or until thick and creamy. Beat in sugar, a tablespoon at a time, until dissolved. Transfer mixture to large bowl. Fold in sifted flour and cocoa, then butter and the hot water.

3 Divide mixture among pan holes. Bake about 12 minutes or until cakes spring back when touched lightly. Turn cakes, top-side up, onto wire rack to cool.

4 Meanwhile, make chocolate ganache.

5 Beat cream and extra sugar in small bowl with electric mixer until soft peaks form. Cut cooled cakes in half. Spread bases with cream; replace tops.

6 Spread chocolate ganache over cakes then sprinkle with coconut.

chocolate ganache Stir ingredients in small saucepan over low heat until smooth. Cool to a spreading consistency.

makes 18
preparation time 35 minutes
cooking time 15 minutes

choc top

125g butter, softened, chopped
1 teaspoon vanilla extract
⅔ cup (150g) caster sugar
3 eggs
1½ cups (225g)
    self-raising flour
¼ cup (60ml) milk
100g dark eating
    chocolate, melted
100g white eating
    chocolate, melted
dark chocolate ganache
125g dark eating chocolate,
    chopped coarsely
⅓ cup (80ml)
    thickened cream

1 Preheat oven to 180°C/160°C fan-forced.
Line deep 12-hole patty pans with paper cases.
2 Combine butter, extract, sugar, eggs,
flour and milk in small bowl of electric mixer;
beat on low speed until ingredients are just
combined. Increase speed to medium; beat
about 3 minutes or until mixture is smooth
and changed to a paler colour.
3 Divide mixture among cases; bake about
20 minutes. Turn cakes, top-side up, onto
wire rack to cool.
4 Meanwhile, make dark chocolate ganache.
5 Spread melted chocolates separately onto
a cold surface; when set, drag a melon baller
over the chocolate to make curls.
6 Spread top of cakes with dark chocolate
ganache. Arrange chocolate curls on top
of cakes.
dark chocolate ganache Stir ingredients in
small saucepan over low heat until smooth.
Cool to a spreading consistency.

makes 24
preparation time 30 minutes
cooking time 20 minutes

chocolate ginger cakes with honeycomb cream

½ cup (110g) firmly packed
   brown sugar
½ cup (75g) plain flour
½ cup (75g) self-raising flour
¼ teaspoon bicarbonate
   of soda
1 teaspoon ground ginger
½ teaspoon ground cinnamon
¼ teaspoon ground nutmeg
90g butter, softened, chopped
1 egg
¼ cup (60ml) buttermilk
2 tablespoons golden syrup
50g dark eating chocolate,
   chopped coarsely
300ml thickened cream,
   whipped
3 x 50g Violet Crumble bars,
   chopped coarsely

1 Preheat oven to 160°C/140°C fan-forced. Line 6-hole texas (¾-cup/180ml) or 12-hole standard (⅓-cup/80ml) muffin pan with paper cases.

2 Sift dry ingredients into small bowl of electric mixer; add butter, egg, buttermilk and syrup. Beat on low speed until ingredients are combined; increase speed to medium, beat until mixture is changed to a paler colour. Stir in chocolate. Divide mixture among cases; smooth surface.

3 Bake large cakes about 40 minutes, small cakes about 30 minutes. Turn cakes, top-side up, onto wire rack to cool.

4 Spread cakes with whipped cream; top with honeycomb.

makes 6 large cakes or 12 small cakes
preparation time 30 minutes
cooking time large cakes 40 minutes; small cakes 30 minutes

6

black forest cakes

425g can pitted cherries
in syrup
165g butter, chopped
100g dark eating chocolate,
chopped coarsely
1⅓ cups (295g) caster sugar
¼ cup (60ml) cherry brandy
1 cup (150g) plain flour
2 tablespoons
self-raising flour
2 tablespoons cocoa powder
1 egg
⅔ cup (160ml) thickened
cream, whipped
2 teaspoons cherry
brandy, extra
100g dark eating chocolate,
left whole

1 Preheat oven to 160°C/140°C fan-forced. Line 6-hole texas (¾-cup/180ml) or 12-hole standard (⅓-cup/80ml) muffin pan with paper cases.

2 Drain cherries; reserve syrup. Process ½ cup cherries with ½ cup syrup until smooth. Halve remaining cherries; reserve for decorating cakes. Discard remaining syrup.

3 Combine butter, chocolate, sugar, brandy and cherry puree in small saucepan; stir over low heat until chocolate is melted. Transfer mixture to medium bowl; cool 15 minutes.

4 Whisk in sifted flours and cocoa, then egg. Divide mixture among cases; smooth surface.

5 Bake large cakes about 55 minutes, small cakes about 45 minutes. Turn cakes, top-side up, onto wire rack to cool.

6 Combine cream and extra cherry brandy in small bowl. Top cakes with remaining cherry halves then brandy cream. Using sharp vegetable peeler, scrape down the long side of chocolate to make small chocolate curls; sprinkle over cakes.

makes 6 large cakes or 12 small cakes
preparation time 35 minutes
(plus cooling time)
cooking time large cakes 55 minutes;
small cakes 45 minutes
tip The chocolate will curl much easier if it is at room temperature.

lamington angel cakes

90g butter, softened
½ teaspoon vanilla extract
½ cup (110g) caster sugar
2 eggs
1 cup (150g) self-raising flour
2 tablespoons milk
1 cup (80g) desiccated
   coconut
¼ cup (80g) raspberry jam
½ cup (125ml) thickened
   cream, whipped
chocolate icing
10g butter
⅓ cup (80ml) milk
2 cups (320g) icing sugar
¼ cup (25g) cocoa powder

1 Preheat oven to 180°C/160°C fan-forced.
Line 6-hole texas (¾-cup/180ml) or 12-hole
standard (⅓-cup/80ml) muffin pan with
paper cases.
2 Combine butter, extract, sugar, eggs, flour
and milk in small bowl of electric mixer; beat on
low speed until ingredients are just combined.
Increase speed to medium; beat until mixture
is changed to a paler colour.
3 Divide mixture among cases; smooth
surface.   Bake large cakes about 25 minutes,
small cakes about 20 minutes. Turn cakes,
top-side up, onto wire rack to cool.
4 Meanwhile, make chocolate icing.
5 Remove cases from cakes. Dip cakes in
chocolate icing; drain off excess, toss cakes
in coconut. Stand cakes on wire rack to set.
6 Cut cakes as desired; fill with jam and cream.
chocolate icing Melt butter in medium
heatproof bowl over medium saucepan
of simmering water. Stir in milk and sifted
icing sugar and cocoa until icing is of a
coating consistency.

makes 6 large cakes or 12 small cakes
preparation time 35 minutes
(plus standing time)
cooking time large cakes 25 minutes;
small cakes 20 minutes

chocolate date and almond meringues

6 egg whites
1½ cups (330g) caster sugar
2 teaspoons 100% corn cornflour
1 cup (150g) finely chopped dried dates
150g dark eating chocolate, chopped finely
1 cup (160g) almond kernels, roasted, chopped coarsely
125g dark eating chocolate, extra, melted
20 almond kernels, extra

1 Preheat oven to 140°C/120°C fan-forced. Line 20 holes of two 12-hole standard (⅓-cup/80ml) muffin pans with paper cases.
2 Beat egg whites in large bowl with electric mixer until soft peaks form; gradually add sugar, beat until dissolved between additions. Gently and quickly fold in cornflour, dates, chocolate and chopped nuts.
3 Divide mixture among cases. Bake about 50 minutes or until dry to touch. Cool in oven with door ajar.
4 Spread tops with melted chocolate; top each meringue with an extra almond. Stand until set.

makes 20
preparation time 20 minutes (plus cooling and standing time)
cooking time 50 minutes

coffee caramel cakes

125g butter, softened, chopped
⅔ cup (150g) firmly packed
   brown sugar
2 tablespoons ground coffee
1 tablespoon boiling water
2 eggs
2 cups (300g) self-raising flour
½ cup (125ml) milk
18 jersey caramels, halved
1 tablespoon icing sugar

1 Preheat oven to 180°C/160°C fan-forced. Line 12-hole standard (⅓-cup/80ml) muffin pan with paper cases.

2 Beat butter and sugar in small bowl with electric mixer until light and fluffy. Add combined coffee and water, then beat in eggs, one at a time, beating until just combined between additions. Transfer mixture to large bowl.

3 Stir in sifted flour and milk. Divide mixture among cases. Press three caramel halves into the centre of each cake; cover with batter. Bake about 20 minutes or until browned.

4 Stand cakes in pan 5 minutes before turning, top-side up, onto wire rack to cool. Serve dusted with sifted icing sugar.

makes 12
preparation time 15 minutes
cooking time 20 minutes

caramel mud cakes

125g butter, chopped
100g white eating chocolate,
    chopped coarsely
⅔ cup (150g) firmly packed
    brown sugar
¼ cup (90g) golden syrup
⅔ cup (160ml) milk
1 cup (150g) plain flour
⅓ cup (50g) self-raising flour
1 egg
½ cup (80g) icing sugar

1 Preheat oven to 160°C/140°C fan-forced. Line 6-hole texas (¾-cup/180ml) or 12-hole standard (⅓-cup/80ml) muffin pan with paper cases.
2 Combine butter, chocolate, sugar, syrup and milk in small saucepan; stir over low heat until smooth. Transfer mixture to medium bowl; cool 15 minutes.
3 Whisk sifted flours then egg into chocolate mixture. Divide mixture among cases.
4 Bake large cakes about 40 minutes, small cakes about 30 minutes. Turn cakes, top-side up, onto wire rack to cool.
5 Place doily, lace or stencil over cake; sift a little icing sugar over doily, then carefully lift doily from cake. Repeat with remaining cakes and icing sugar.

makes 6 large cakes or 12 small cakes
preparation time 25 minutes
(plus cooling time)
cooking time large cakes 40 minutes; small cakes 30 minutes
tip You need a doily, lace or a stencil to decorate the cakes. The best decorating result is achieved by using several doilies still joined together, pieces of plastic-backed lace tablecloths or thick fabric lace, as they are easier to lift away from the cake once dusted with icing sugar.

white chocolate mud cakes

250g butter, chopped
150g white eating chocolate,
    chopped coarsely
2 cups (440g) caster sugar
1 cup (250ml) milk
1½ cups (225g) plain flour
½ cup (75g) self-raising flour
1 teaspoon vanilla extract
2 eggs, beaten lightly
small flowers
silver cachous
fluffy frosting
1 cup (220g) caster sugar
⅓ cup (80ml) water
2 egg whites

makes 24 cakes
preparation time 1 hour
(plus cooling time)
cooking time 40 minutes
tip For a soft frosting of
marshmallow consistency, ice
cakes on the day of serving as
the following day the frosting
will lose its gloss. Add flowers
a few hours ahead, or very
delicate flowers as close to
serving a possible.

1 Preheat oven to 160°C/140°C fan-forced.
Line two 12-hole standard (⅓-cup/80ml)
muffin pans with paper cases.
2 Combine butter, chocolate, sugar and milk
in medium saucepan; stir over low heat,
without boiling, until smooth. Transfer mixture
to medium bowl; cool 15 minutes.
3 Whisk sifted flours, then extract and egg
into chocolate mixture. Divide mixture among
cases; bake about 35 minutes. Turn cakes,
top-side up, onto wire rack to cool.
4 Make fluffy frosting.
5 Spread cakes with fluffy frosting; decorate
with flowers and cachous.

fluffy frosting Combine sugar and the water
in small saucepan; stir over low heat, without
boiling, until sugar dissolves. Bring to a boil; boil,
uncovered, without stirring, about 3 minutes or
until syrup is slightly thick. Remove syrup from
heat, allow bubbles to subside. Test the syrup
by dropping 1 teaspoon of it into cold water. The
syrup should form a ball of soft sticky toffee
when rolled between fingertips (114°C on a
sugar thermometer). The syrup should not colour;
if it does, discard it. Just before syrup reaches
the correct temperature, beat egg whites in a
small bowl with electric mixer until firm. When
syrup is ready, allow bubbles to subside then,
with electric mixer operating on medium speed,
pour a thin stream of syrup onto egg whites. If
syrup is added too quickly to the egg whites,
frosting will not thicken. Continue to beat on
high speed about 5 minutes or until thick.
Frosting should be barely warm by now.

coconut cherry hearts

125g butter, softened, chopped
½ teaspoon coconut essence
⅔ cup (150g) caster sugar
2 eggs
⅓ cup (80ml) milk
½ cup (40g)
    desiccated coconut
⅓ cup (70g) red glacé cherries,
    chopped coarsely
50g dark eating chocolate,
    chopped coarsely
1 cup (150g) self-raising flour
¼ cup (35g) plain flour
150g white chocolate
    Melts, melted
pink food colouring
milk chocolate ganache
¼ cup (60ml) cream
100g milk eating chocolate,
    chopped coarsely

1 Preheat oven to 180°C/160°C fan-forced. Line 6-hole texas (¾-cup/180ml) or 12-hole standard (⅓-cup/80ml) muffin pan with paper cases.
2 Beat butter, essence, sugar and eggs in small bowl with electric mixer until combined.
3 Stir in milk, coconut, cherries and chocolate, then sifted flours. Divide mixture among cases; smooth surface.
4 Bake large cakes about 35 minutes, small cakes about 25 minutes. Turn cakes, top-side up, onto wire rack to cool.
5 Meanwhile, make milk chocolate ganache.
6 Divide white chocolate evenly among three small bowls; tint two portions in two different shades of pink.
7 Pipe different coloured heart shapes onto baking-paper-lined oven tray. Stand at room temperature until set.
8 Spread cakes with ganache; decorate with coloured hearts.

milk chocolate ganache Stir ingredients in small saucepan over low heat until smooth. Cool to a spreading consistency.

makes 6 large cakes or 12 small cakes
preparation time 35 minutes
(plus standing time)
cooking time large cakes 35 minutes; small cakes 25 minutes
tip To tint chocolate it is best to use a skewer; add a few drops of colouring into melted chocolate and stir with a clean dry spoon until colour is even.

21

apple custard teacakes

90g butter, softened, chopped
½ teaspoon vanilla extract
½ cup (110g) caster sugar
2 eggs
¾ cup (110g) self-raising flour
¼ cup (30g) custard powder
2 tablespoons milk
1 large unpeeled apple (200g),
  cored, sliced thinly
30g butter, melted
1 tablespoon caster
  sugar, extra
½ teaspoon ground
  cinnamon

custard

1 tablespoon custard powder
1 tablespoon caster sugar
½ cup (125ml) milk
¼ teaspoon vanilla extract

1 Make custard.

2 Preheat oven to 180°C/160°C fan-forced. Line 6-hole texas (¾-cup/180ml) or 12-hole standard (⅓-cup/80ml) muffin pan with paper cases.

3 Combine butter, extract, sugar, eggs, sifted flour and custard powder, and milk in small bowl of electric mixer; beat on low speed until ingredients are just combined. Increase speed to medium; beat until mixture is changed to a paler colour.

4 Divide half the mixture among cases. Top with custard, then remaining cake mixture; spread mixture to cover custard. Top with apple slices, pressing slightly into cake.

5 Bake large cakes about 40 minutes, small cakes about 30 minutes.

6 Brush hot cakes with extra butter, then sprinkle with combined extra sugar and cinnamon. Turn cakes, top-side up, onto wire rack to cool.

custard Blend custard powder and sugar with milk and extract in small saucepan; stir over heat until mixture boils and thickens. Remove from heat; cover surface with plastic wrap; cool.

makes 6 large cakes or 12 small cakes
preparation time 30 minutes
(plus cooling time)
cooking time large cakes 40 minutes;
small cakes 30 minutes

passionfruit curd cakes

90g butter, softened
½ cup (110g) caster sugar
2 eggs
1 cup (150g) self-raising flour
¼ cup (60ml) passionfruit pulp
85g packet passionfruit jelly
1 cup (250ml) boiling water
1 cup (80g) desiccated
   coconut
½ cup (125ml) thickened
   cream, whipped
passionfruit curd
2 eggs, beaten lightly
⅓ cup (75g) caster sugar
1 tablespoon lemon juice
¼ cup (60ml) passionfruit pulp
60g butter, chopped coarsely

1 Make passionfruit curd.

2 Meanwhile, preheat oven to 180°C/160°C fan-forced. Line 6-hole texas (¾-cup/180ml) or 12-hole standard (⅓-cup/80ml) muffin pan with paper cases.

3 Combine butter, sugar, eggs and flour in small bowl of electric mixer; beat on low speed until ingredients are just combined. Increase speed to medium; beat until mixture is changed to a paler colour. Stir in passionfruit pulp.

4 Divide mixture among cases; smooth surface. Bake large cakes about 25 minutes, small cakes about 20 minutes. Turn cakes, top-side up, onto wire rack to cool.

5 Dissolve jelly in the boiling water. Refrigerate about 30 minutes or until set to the consistency of unbeaten egg white.

6 Remove cases from cakes. Roll cakes in jelly; leave cakes to stand in jelly for 15 minutes turning occasionally. Roll cakes in coconut; place on wire rack over tray. Refrigerate 30 minutes.

7 Cut cakes in half; fill with curd and cream.

passionfruit curd Combine ingredients in small heatproof bowl. Place over small saucepan of simmering water; stir constantly until mixture thickens slightly and coats the back of a spoon. Remove from heat. Cover tightly; refrigerate curd until cold.

makes 6 large cakes or 12 small cakes
preparation time 35 minutes
(plus refrigeration and standing time)
cooking time large cakes 25 minutes;
small cakes 20 minutes

25

veryberry cakes

125g butter, softened, chopped
½ teaspoon vanilla extract
⅔ cup (150g) caster sugar
2 eggs
1 cup (150g) dried
 mixed berries
½ cup (70g) slivered almonds
⅔ cup (100g) plain flour
⅓ cup (50g) self-raising flour
¼ cup (60ml) milk
sugared fruit
150g fresh blueberries
120g fresh raspberries
1 egg white, beaten lightly
2 tablespoons vanilla sugar
cream cheese frosting
30g butter, softened
80g cream cheese, softened
1½ cups (240g) icing sugar

1 Prepare sugared fruit.
2 Preheat oven to 160°C/140°C fan-forced. Line 6-hole texas (¾-cup/180ml) or 12-hole standard (⅓-cup/80ml) muffin pan with paper cases.
3 Beat butter, extract, sugar and eggs in small bowl with electric mixer until light and fluffy. Stir in fruit and nuts, then sifted flours and milk.
4 Divide mixture among cases; smooth surface. Bake large cakes about 45 minutes, small cakes about 35 minutes. Turn cakes, top-side up, onto wire rack to cool.
5 Make cream cheese frosting.
6 Spread cakes with frosting; decorate with sugared fruit.

sugared fruit Brush each berry lightly with egg white; roll fruit in vanilla sugar. Place fruit on baking-paper-lined tray. Leave about 1 hour or until sugar is dry.

cream cheese frosting Beat butter and cream cheese in small bowl with electric mixer until light and fluffy; gradually beat in sifted icing sugar.

makes 6 large cakes or 12 small cakes
preparation time 40 minutes
(plus standing time)
cooking time large cakes 45 minutes; small cakes 35 minutes

daisy cakes

125g butter, softened, chopped
1 teaspoon vanilla extract
⅔ cup (150g) caster sugar
3 eggs
1½ cups (225g)
    self-raising flour
¼ cup (60ml) milk
60 pink marshmallows
24 red smarties
vanilla butter cream
125g butter, softened, chopped
1 teaspoon vanilla extract
1½ cups (240g) icing sugar
2 tablespoons milk

1 Preheat oven to 180°C/160°C fan-forced. Line two 12-hole patty pans with paper cases.
2 Combine butter, extract, sugar, eggs, sifted flour and milk in small bowl of electric mixer; beat on low speed until ingredients are just combined. Increase speed to medium; beat about 3 minutes or until mixture is smooth and changed to a paler colour.
3 Divide mixture among cases; bake about 20 minutes. Turn cakes, top-side up, onto wire rack to cool.
4 Meanwhile, make vanilla butter cream.
5 Spread tops of cakes with butter cream. Cut marshmallows in half horizontally; squeeze ends together to form petals. Decorate cakes with petals; position a smartie in the centre of each daisy.

vanilla butter cream Beat butter and extract in small bowl with electric mixer until as white as possible. Gradually beat in half the sifted icing sugar, milk, then remaining icing sugar.

makes 24
preparation time 30 minutes
cooking time 20 minutes

melt-in-the-mouth vanilla biscuits

180g butter, softened, chopped
1 teaspoon vanilla bean paste
1 cup (160g) icing sugar
1½ tablespoons milk
1¾ cups (260g) plain flour
2 tablespoons cornflour

1 Beat butter, vanilla and ⅓ cup sifted icing sugar in small bowl with electric mixer until light and fluffy. Add milk; beat until combined. Add sifted flour and cornflour; beat on low speed until combined.
2 Refrigerate biscuit dough about 10 minutes or until firm enough to roll.
3 Roll dough into a 30cm log; wrap in plastic. Refrigerate dough 1 hour.
4 Preheat oven to 160°C/140°C fan-forced. Grease oven trays.
5 Cut dough into 4mm slices. Place slices on trays 3cm apart. Bake about 10 minutes or until just golden. Stand biscuits on trays 5 minutes before transferring to wire racks to cool slightly.
6 While still warm, dust biscuits liberally with remaining sifted icing sugar. Cool completely on wire racks.

makes 60
preparation time 20 minutes (plus refrigeration and cooling time)
cooking time 10 minutes per tray
tips Store in an airtight container at room temperature for up to one week.
You can substitute the vanilla paste with 3 teaspoons vanilla extract, if you prefer.

chewy choc-chunk cookies

2 eggs
1⅓ cups (295g) firmly packed brown sugar
1 teaspoon vanilla extract
1 cup (150g) plain flour
¾ cup (110g) self-raising flour
½ teaspoon bicarbonate of soda
½ cup (125ml) vegetable oil
1 cup (120g) coarsely chopped roasted pecans
¾ cup (120g) coarsely chopped raisins
1 cup (150g) dark chocolate Melts, halved
½ cup (95g) white Choc Bits

1 Beat eggs, sugar and extract in small bowl with electric mixer about 1 minute or until mixture becomes lighter in colour.
2 Stir in sifted dry ingredients then remaining ingredients (the mixture will be soft). Cover bowl; refrigerate 1 hour.
3 Preheat oven to 200°C/180°C fan-forced. Grease oven trays.
4 Roll heaped tablespoons of mixture into balls; place on trays 6cm apart, flatten into 6cm rounds.
5 Bake about 10 minutes or until browned lightly. Stand cookies on trays 5 minutes before transferring to wire racks to cool.

makes 20
preparation time 25 minutes (plus refrigeration time)
cooking time 10 minutes per tray
tips Store in an airtight container at room temperature for up to one week. Walnuts can be substituted for pecans, if desired.

triple-choc cookies

125g butter, softened, chopped
½ teaspoon vanilla extract
1¼ cups (275g) firmly packed brown sugar
1 egg
1 cup (150g) plain flour
¼ cup (35g) self-raising flour
1 teaspoon bicarbonate of soda
⅓ cup (35g) cocoa powder
½ cup (85g) coarsely chopped raisins
½ cup (95g) milk Choc Bits
½ cup (75g) white chocolate Melts, halved
½ cup (75g) dark chocolate Melts, halved

1 Preheat oven to 180°C/160°C fan-forced. Grease oven trays.
2 Beat butter, extract, sugar and egg in small bowl with electric mixer until smooth; do not overbeat. Stir in sifted dry ingredients, then raisins and all the chocolate.
3 Drop level tablespoons of mixture onto trays, allowing 5cm between each cookie; bake about 10 minutes. Stand cookies 5 minutes before transferring to wire rack to cool.

makes 36
preparation time 10 minutes
cooking time 10 minutes per tray
tips For a firmer cookie, bake an extra 2 minutes.
Cookies can be stored in an airtight container at room temperature for up to one week.

chocolate lace crisps

100g dark eating chocolate, chopped coarsely
80g butter, chopped
1 cup (220g) caster sugar
1 egg, beaten lightly
1 cup (150g) plain flour
2 tablespoons cocoa powder
¼ teaspoon bicarbonate of soda
¼ cup (40g) icing sugar

1 Melt chocolate and butter in small saucepan over low heat. Transfer to medium bowl.
2 Stir in caster sugar, egg and sifted flour, cocoa and soda. Cover; refrigerate about 15 minutes or until mixture is firm enough to handle.
3 Meanwhile, preheat oven to 180°C/160°C fan-forced. Grease oven trays; line with baking paper.
4 Roll level tablespoons of mixture into balls; roll each ball in icing sugar, place on trays 8cm apart. Bake about 15 minutes; cool crisps on trays.

makes 24
preparation time 25 minutes (plus refrigeration time)
cooking time 20 minutes per tray
tip Store in an airtight container at room temperature for up to one week.

coffee snaps

125g butter, softened, chopped
1¼ cups (275g) firmly packed brown sugar
3 teaspoons ground coffee
½ teaspoon vanilla extract
1 egg
¾ cup (110g) plain flour
¾ cup (110g) self-raising flour
2 tablespoons (70g) coffee beans (70 beans)

1 Preheat oven to 180°C/160°C fan-forced. Grease oven trays.
2 Beat butter, sugar, coffee and extract in small bowl with electric mixer until pale and fluffy. Add egg; beat until just combined. Stir in sifted flours.
3 Roll rounded teaspoons of mixture into balls; place on trays 3cm apart, top each with a coffee bean.
4 Bake about 10 minutes or until browned. Stand 5 minutes before transferring to wire rack to cool.

makes 70
preparation time 15 minutes
cooking time 10 minutes per tray
tip Store in an airtight container at room temperature for up to one week.

hazelnut pinwheels

1¼ cups (175g) plain flour
100g butter, chopped
½ cup (110g) caster sugar
1 egg yolk
1 tablespoon milk, approximately
⅓ cup (110g) chocolate hazelnut spread
2 tablespoons hazelnut meal

1 Process flour, butter and sugar until crumbly. Add egg yolk; process with enough milk until mixture forms a ball. Knead dough on floured surface until smooth; cover, refrigerate 1 hour.
2 Roll dough between sheets of baking paper to form 20cm x 30cm rectangle; remove top sheet of paper. Spread dough evenly with hazelnut spread; sprinkle with hazelnut meal. Using paper as a guide, roll dough tightly from long side to enclose filling. Enclose roll in plastic wrap; refrigerate 30 minutes.
3 Meanwhile, preheat oven to 180°C/160°C fan-forced. Grease oven trays; line with baking paper.
4 Remove plastic wrap; cut roll into 1cm slices, place slices on trays 2cm apart. Bake about 20 minutes. Stand pinwheels on trays 5 minutes before transferring to wire rack to cool.

makes 30
preparation time 20 minutes (plus refrigeration time)
cooking time 20 minutes per tray
tip Store in an airtight container at room temperature for up to one week.

snickerdoodles

250g butter, softened, chopped
1 teaspoon vanilla extract
½ cup (110g) firmly packed brown sugar
1 cup (220g) caster sugar
2 eggs
2¾ cups (410g) plain flour
1 teaspoon bicarbonate of soda
½ teaspoon ground nutmeg
1 tablespoon caster sugar, extra
2 teaspoons ground cinnamon

1 Beat butter, extract and sugars in small bowl with electric mixer until light and fluffy. Add eggs, one at a time, beating until just combined. Transfer to large bowl.
2 Stir combined sifted flour, soda and nutmeg, in two batches, into egg mixture. Cover; refrigerate dough 30 minutes.
3 Preheat oven to 180°C/160°C fan-forced.
4 Combine extra caster sugar and cinnamon in small shallow bowl. Roll level tablespoons of the dough into balls; roll balls in cinnamon sugar. Place balls on ungreased oven trays, 7cm apart. Bake about 12 minutes; cool biscuits on trays.

makes 50
preparation time 25 minutes (plus refrigeration time)
cooking time 12 minutes per tray
tip Store in an airtight container at room temperature for up to one week.

pistachio shortbread mounds

½ cup (75g) shelled pistachios
250g butter, softened, chopped
1 cup (160g) icing sugar
1½ cups (225g) plain flour
2 tablespoons rice flour
2 tablespoons cornflour
¾ cup (90g) almond meal
⅓ cup (55g) icing sugar, extra

1 Preheat oven to 150°C/130°C fan-forced. Grease oven trays.
2 Toast nuts in small heavy-based frying pan until browned lightly; remove from pan. Coarsely chop ⅓ cup of the nuts; leave remaining nuts whole.
3 Beat butter and icing sugar in small bowl with electric mixer until light and fluffy; transfer mixture to large bowl. Stir in sifted flours, almond meal and chopped nuts.
4 Shape level tablespoons of mixture into mounds; place mounds on trays 3cm apart. Press one reserved nut onto each mound.
5 Bake about 25 minutes or until firm. Stand mounds 5 minutes before transferring to wire rack to cool.
6 Serve mounds dusted with extra sifted icing sugar.

makes 40
preparation time 25 minutes
cooking time 25 minutes per tray

stained-glass Christmas cookies

250g butter, softened, chopped

2 teaspoons finely grated
   lemon rind

½ teaspoon almond essence

¾ cup (165g) caster sugar

1 egg

1 tablespoon water

2¼ cups (335g) plain flour

90g individually wrapped
   sugar-free fruit drops,
   assorted colours

1 Beat butter, rind, essence, sugar, egg and the water in small bowl with electric mixer until smooth (do not overbeat). Transfer mixture to large bowl; stir in flour. Knead dough on floured surface until smooth. Cover with plastic wrap; refrigerate 30 minutes.

2 Meanwhile, using rolling pin, gently tap wrapped lollies to crush slightly. Unwrap lollies; separate by colour into small bowls.

3 Preheat oven to 180°C/160°C fan-forced. Grease oven trays; line with baking paper.

4 Roll dough between sheets of baking paper until 4mm thick. Cut shapes from dough using medium-sized cookie cutters; use very small cookie cutters to cut out centre of each cookie.

5 Place cookies on trays; bake about 5 minutes. Remove trays from oven; fill cut-out centre of each cookie with crushed lollies. Return to oven for 5 minutes. Cool cookies on trays.

makes about 36

preparation time 1 hour
(plus refrigeration time)

cooking time 10 minutes per tray

tip Use traditional Christmas cutters such as trees, stars, angels, etc, when cutting out the cookie shapes, and smaller versions of the same shapes for the "stained-glass" centre holes. If you wish, make a small hole near the top of each cookie through which, after the baked cookie has cooled, you can thread a ribbon to turn the cookie into a Christmas tree decoration.

crunchy muesli cookies

1 cup (90g) rolled oats
1 cup (150g) plain flour
1 cup (220g) caster sugar
2 teaspoons ground cinnamon
¼ cup (35g) craisins
⅓ cup (55g) finely chopped dried apricots
½ cup (70g) slivered almonds
125g butter
2 tablespoons golden syrup
½ teaspoon bicarbonate of soda
1 tablespoon boiling water

1 Preheat oven to 150°C/130°C fan-forced. Grease oven trays; line with baking paper.
2 Combine oats, flour, sugar, cinnamon, dried fruit and nuts in large bowl.
3 Melt butter with golden syrup in small saucepan over low heat; add combined soda and the boiling water. Stir warm butter mixture into dry ingredients.
4 Roll level tablespoons of mixture into balls, place on trays 5cm apart; flatten with hand. Bake about 20 minutes; cool cookies on trays.

makes 36
preparation time 15 minutes
cooking time 25 minutes per tray
tip Store in an airtight container at room temperature for up to one week.

almond jam cookies

185g butter, softened, chopped
1 teaspoon vanilla extract
¾ cup (165g) caster sugar
2 egg yolks
½ cup (60g) almond meal
1½ cups (225g) plain flour
½ teaspoon baking power
2 tablespoons apricot jam, approximately
1 teaspoon grated lemon rind
2 tablespoons raspberry jam, approximately

1 Preheat oven to 160°C/140°C fan-forced.
2 Beat butter, extract, sugar and egg yolks in medium bowl with electric mixer until just combined. Stir in almond meal, flour and baking powder; mix well. Roll level tablespoons of mixture into balls; place on ungreased oven trays 5cm apart.
3 Press a hollow into each ball about 1cm deep and 1.5cm wide using the handle of a lightly floured wooden spoon.
4 Combine apricot jam with half of the rind. Combine raspberry jam with remaining rind. Carefully spoon a little apricot jam into half the cookies; spoon raspberry jam into remaining cookies.
5 Bake about 25 minutes; cool cookies on trays.

makes 30
preparation time 35 minutes
cooking time 25 minutes per tray
tips If jam sinks during cooking, top up with a little extra, if desired. Store in an airtight container at room temperature for up to three weeks.

oat and bran biscuits

1 cup (150g) plain flour
1 cup (70g) unprocessed bran
¾ cup (65g) rolled oats
½ teaspoon bicarbonate of soda
60g butter, chopped
½ cup (110g) caster sugar
1 egg
2 tablespoons water, approximately

1 Process flour, bran, oats, soda and butter until crumbly; add sugar, egg and enough of the water to make a firm dough. Knead dough on floured surface until smooth; cover, refrigerate 30 minutes.
2 Preheat oven to 180°C/160°C fan-forced. Grease oven trays; line with baking paper.
3 Divide dough in half; roll each half between sheets of baking paper to about 5mm thickness. Cut dough into 7cm rounds; place on trays 2cm apart.
4 Bake about 15 minutes. Stand biscuits on trays 5 minutes before transferring to wire rack to cool.

makes 30
preparation time 15 minutes (plus refrigeration time)
cooking time 15 minutes per tray
tip Store in an airtight container at room temperature for up to one week.

polenta and orange biscuits

125g butter, softened, chopped
2 teaspoons finely grated orange rind
⅔ cup (110g) icing sugar
⅓ cup (55g) polenta
1 cup (150g) plain flour

1 Preheat oven to 180°C/160°C fan-forced. Grease oven trays; line with baking paper.
2 Beat butter, rind and sifted icing sugar in small bowl with electric mixer until just combined; stir in polenta and sifted flour. Shape mixture into 30cm-rectangular log; cut log into 1cm slices.
3 Place slices on trays 2cm apart; bake about 15 minutes. Stand biscuits on trays 5 minutes before transferring to wire rack to cool.

makes 30
preparation time 15 minutes
cooking time 15 minutes per tray
tip Store in an airtight container at room temperature for up to one week.

passionfruit
butter
biscuits

passionfruit butter biscuits

250g butter, softened
1⅓ cups (220g) icing sugar
2 cups (300g) plain flour
½ cup (75g) cornflour
⅓ cup (65g) rice flour
2 tablespoons passionfruit pulp

1 Combine butter, sugar and flours in large bowl of food processor; process 2 minutes or until mixture is combined. Add passionfruit; process until mixture clings together.
2 Transfer mixture to floured surface; knead gently until smooth. Divide dough in half, roll each half into 26cm log; wrap in plastic. Refrigerate 1 hour.
3 Preheat oven to 160°C/140°C fan-forced. Grease oven trays.
4 Cut logs into 1cm slices; place slices on trays 3cm apart. Bake about 20 minutes. Stand biscuits on trays 5 minutes before transferring to wire rack to cool.

makes 40
preparation time 25 minutes (plus refrigeration time)
cooking time 20 minutes per tray
tip Store in an airtight container at room temperature for up to one week.

almond crisps

125g butter, softened, chopped
¼ cup (55g) caster sugar
1 cup (150g) self-raising flour
¼ cup (30g) almond meal
2 tablespoons flaked almonds

1 Preheat oven to 200°C/180°C fan-forced. Grease oven trays.
2 Beat butter and sugar in small bowl with electric mixer until smooth.
Stir in flour and almond meal.
3 Roll level tablespoons of mixture into balls; place on trays 5cm apart.
Flatten slightly with floured fork to 1cm thick; sprinkle with flaked almonds.
4 Bake about 10 minutes. Stand crisps on trays 5 minutes before
transferring to wire racks to cool.

makes 15
preparation time 25 minutes
cooking time 10 minutes per tray
tip Store in an airtight container at room temperature for up to two weeks.

glossary

almonds flat, pointy-tipped nuts having a pitted brown shell enclosing a creamy white kernel that is covered by a brown skin.

meal nuts are powdered to a coarse flour texture for use in baking or as a thickening agent; also known as ground almonds.

flaked paper-thin slices.

slivered small pieces cut lengthways.

bicarbonate of soda also known as baking soda.

butter unless stated otherwise, this book uses salted butter; 125g is equal to 1 stick (4 ounces).

buttermilk in spite of its name, buttermilk is actually low in fat; originally the term given to the slightly sour liquid left after butter was churned from cream, today it is made similarly to yogurt. It is available from the dairy department in supermarkets.

cachous also called dragées; minuscule (3mm to 5mm) metallic-looking, but edible, confectionery balls used in cake decorating.

chocolate

Choc Bits also known as chocolate chips or chocolate morsels; hold their shape in baking and are ideal for decorating.

dark eating also known as semi-sweet; made of a high percentage of cocoa liquor, cocoa butter and sugar.

hazelnut spread a thick smooth paste made from chocolate and hazelnuts.

Melts small discs of compounded milk, white or dark chocolate; ideal for melting and moulding.

milk eating most popular eating chocolate; mild and very sweet.

white eating contains no cocoa solids but derives its sweet flavour from cocoa butter. Sensitive to heat.

cinnamon available both in sticks (or quills) and ground; one of the world's most common spices. Used universally as a sweet, fragrant flavouring for both sweet and savoury foods.

cocoa powder also known as unsweetened cocoa; cocoa beans (cacao seeds) that have been fermented, roasted, shelled, ground into powder then cleared of most of the fat content.

coconut

desiccated concentrated, dried, unsweetened and shredded coconut flesh.

flaked dried flaked coconut flesh.

cornflour also known as cornstarch. Made from either wheat or corn.

craisins dried sweetened cranberries; used in sweet or savoury dishes. Can usually be substituted for, or with, other dried fruit in most recipes.

cream cheese also known as Philadelphia or Philly; a soft cow-milk cheese. Also available as a "light" cream cheese, which is a blend of cottage and cream cheese.

custard powder instant mixture used to make pouring custard; similar to North American instant pudding mixes.

eggs we use large chicken eggs having an average weight of 60g in our recipes unless stated otherwise.

essence/extract an essence is either a distilled concentration of a food quality or an artificial creation of it. Coconut and almond essences are synthetically produced substances used in small amounts to impart their respective flavours to foods. An *extract* is made by actually extracting the flavour from a food product. In the case of vanilla, pods are soaked, usually in alcohol, to capture the authentic flavour. Both extracts and essences will keep indefinitely if stored in a cool dark place.

flour

plain an all-purpose flour made from wheat.

rice made from ground white rice.

self-raising plain flour sifted with baking powder in the proportion of 1 cup flour to 2 teaspoons baking powder.

ginger, ground also known as powdered ginger; used as a flavouring in cakes, pies and puddings, but cannot be substituted for fresh ginger.

glacé cherries also known as candied cherries; boiled in heavy sugar syrup and then dried. Used in cakes, breads and sweets.

golden syrup a by-product of refined sugarcane; pure maple syrup or honey can be substituted.

hazelnut also known as filberts; plump, grape-sized, rich, sweet nut having a brown skin that is removed by rubbing heated nuts together vigorously in a tea-towel. *Hazelnut meal* is made by grounding the hazelnuts to a coarse flour texture for use in baking or as a thickening agent.

jam also known as preserve or conserve; a thickened mixture of a fruit and sugar.

mascarpone a fresh, unripened, smooth, triple cream cheese with a rich, sweet, slightly acidic, taste.

nutmeg a strong and very pungent spice ground from the dried nut of an evergreen tree native to Indonesia. Usually found ground, but the flavour is more intense from a whole nut, available from spice shops, so it's best to grate your own.

oil

cooking spray we use a cholesterol-free cooking spray made from canola oil.

vegetable any of a number of oils sourced from plants rather than animal fats.

pecans golden brown, rich, buttery nut. Walnuts can be substituted, if preferred.

pine nuts also known as pignoli; not, in fact, a nut, but a small, cream-coloured kernel from pine cones.

pistachios green, delicately flavoured nuts inside hard off-white shells. To peel, soak shelled nuts in boiling water for about 5 minutes; drain, then pat dry with absorbent paper. Rub skins with cloth to peel.

polenta also known as cornmeal; a flour-like cereal made of dried corn (maize). Also the name of the dish made from it.

poppy seeds tiny black seeds with a pungent flavour; store in an airtight container in a cool place or freezer.

raisins dried sweet grapes.

rolled oats flattened oat grain rolled into flakes and traditionally used for porridge. Instant oats are also available, but use traditional oats for baking.

sugar we use coarse, granulated table sugar, also known as crystal sugar, unless otherwise specified.

brown an extremely soft, finely granulated sugar retaining molasses for its colour and flavour.

caster also known as finely granulated or superfine table sugar. The fine crystals dissolve easily, so this sugar is perfect for meringues, cakes and desserts.

icing also known as confectioners' sugar or powdered sugar; pulverised granulated sugar crushed together with a small amount of cornflour.

pure icing also known as confectioners' sugar or powdered sugar.

sultanas dried grapes; also known as golden raisins.

sweetened condensed milk a canned milk product consisting of milk with more than half the water content removed and sugar added to the remaining milk.

sweet sherry fortified wine consumed as an aperitif or used in cooking.

treacle thick, dark syrup not unlike molasses; a by-product of sugar refining. Is more viscous, and has a stronger flavour and aroma than golden syrup.

vanilla sugar sugar that has been flavoured with vanilla.

walnuts is the fruit of the walnut tree; flavourful and rich, it should be stored in the refrigerator because of its high oil content.

conversion chart

MEASURES

One Australian metric measuring cup holds approximately 250ml, one Australian metric tablespoon holds 20ml, one Australian metric teaspoon holds 5ml.

The difference between one country's measuring cups and another's is within a 2- or 3-teaspoon variance, and will not affect your cooking results. North America, New Zealand and the United Kingdom use a 15ml tablespoon. All cup and spoon measurements are level. The most accurate way of measuring dry ingredients is to weigh them. When measuring liquids, use a clear glass or plastic jug with metric markings.

We use large eggs with an average weight of 60g.

DRY MEASURES

METRIC	IMPERIAL
15g	½oz
30g	1oz
60g	2oz
90g	3oz
125g	4oz (¼lb)
155g	5oz
185g	6oz
220g	7oz
250g	8oz (½lb)
280g	9oz
315g	10oz
345g	11oz
375g	12oz (¾lb)
410g	13oz
440g	14oz
470g	15oz
500g	16oz (1lb)
750g	24oz (1½lb)
1kg	32oz (2lb)

LIQUID MEASURES

METRIC	IMPERIAL
30ml	1 fluid oz
60ml	2 fluid oz
100ml	3 fluid oz
125ml	4 fluid oz
150ml	5 fluid oz (¼ pint/1 gill)
190ml	6 fluid oz
250ml	8 fluid oz
300ml	10 fluid oz (½ pint)
500ml	16 fluid oz
600ml	20 fluid oz (1 pint)
1000ml (1 litre)	1¾ pints

LENGTH MEASURES

METRIC	IMPERIAL
3mm	⅛in
6mm	¼in
1cm	½in
2cm	¾in
2.5cm	1in
5cm	2in
6cm	2½in
8cm	3in
10cm	4in
13cm	5in
15cm	6in
18cm	7in
20cm	8in
23cm	9in
25cm	10in
28cm	11in
30cm	12in (1ft)

OVEN TEMPERATURES

These oven temperatures are only a guide for conventional ovens.
For fan-forced ovens, check the manufacturer's manual.

	°C (CELSIUS)	°F (FAHRENHEIT)	GAS MARK
Very slow	120	250	½
Slow	150	275 – 300	1 – 2
Moderately slow	160	325	3
Moderate	180	350 – 375	4 – 5
Moderately hot	200	400	6
Hot	220	425 – 450	7 – 8
Very hot	240	475	9

index

A

almond crisps 58
almond jam cookies 50
apple custard teacakes 22

B

biscuits, melt-in-the-mouth
  vanilla 30
biscuits, oat and bran 53
biscuits, passionfruit butter 57
biscuits, polenta and orange 54
black forest cakes 9
bran and oat biscuits 53
butter biscuits, passionfruit 57
butter cream, vanilla 29

C

caramel coffee cakes 14
caramel mud cakes 17
cherry coconut hearts 21
chewy choc-chunk cookies 33
choc cookies, triple- 34
choc top 5
choc-chunk cookies, chewy 33
chocolate and coconut
  sponge cakes 2
chocolate date and
  almond meringues 13
chocolate ganache 2
chocolate ginger cakes
  with honeycomb cream 6
chocolate icing 10
chocolate lace crisps 37
chocolate, white, mud cakes 18
Christmas cookies,
  stained-glass 46
coconut and chocolate
  sponge cakes 2
coconut cherry hearts 21
coffee caramel cakes 14

coffee snaps 38
cookies, almond jam 50
cookies, chewy choc-chunk 33
cookies, crunchy muesli 49
cookies, stained-glass
  Christmas 46
cookies, triple-choc 34
cream cheese frosting 26
crisps, almond 58
crisps, chocolate lace 37
crunchy muesli cookies 49
curd, passionfruit 25
custard 22

D

daisy cakes 29
dark chocolate ganache 5

F

fluffy frosting 18
frosting, cream cheese 26
frosting, fluffy 18
fruit, sugared 26

G

ganache, chocolate 2
ganache, dark chocolate 5
ganache, milk chocolate 21
ginger chocolate cakes with
  honeycomb cream 6

H

hazelnut pinwheels 41
honeycomb cream with
  chocolate ginger cakes 6

L

lamington angel cakes 10

M

melt-in-the-mouth
  vanilla biscuits 30

meringues, chocolate date
  and almond 13
milk chocolate ganache 21
mud cakes, caramel 17
mud cakes, white chocolate 18
muesli cookies, crunchy 49

O

oat and bran biscuits 53
orange and polenta biscuits 54

P

passionfruit butter biscuits 57
passionfruit curd 25
passionfruit curd cakes 25
pinwheels, hazelnut 41
pistachio shortbread mounds 45
polenta and orange biscuits 54

S

shortbread mounds,
  pistachio 45
snaps, coffee 38
snickerdoodles 42
sponge cakes, chocolate
  and coconut 2
stained-glass
  Christmas cookies 46
sugared fruit 26

T

teacakes, apple custard 22
triple-choc cookies 34

V

vanilla biscuits,
  melt-in-the-mouth 30
vanilla butter cream 29
veryberry cakes 26

W

white chocolate mud cakes 18

Are you missing some of the world's favourite cookbooks?

The Australian Women's Weekly cookbooks are available from bookshops, cookshops, supermarkets and other stores all over the world. You can also buy direct from the publisher, using the order form below.

MINI SERIES £3.50 190x138MM 64 PAGES

TITLE	QTY	TITLE	QTY	TITLE	QTY
4 Fast Ingredients		Fast Soup		Potatoes	
15-minute Feasts		Finger Food		Roast	
50 Fast Chicken Fillets		Gluten-free Cooking		Salads	
50 Fast Desserts		Healthy Everyday Food 4 Kids		Simple Slices	
After-work Stir-fries		Ice-creams & Sorbets		Simply Seafood	
Barbecue Chicken		Indian Cooking		Skinny Food	
Biscuits, Brownies & Biscotti		Indonesian Favourites		Spanish Favourites	
Bites		Italian Favourites		Stir-fries	
Bowl Food		Jams & Jellies		Summer Salads	
Burgers, Rösti & Fritters		Japanese Favourites		Tagines & Couscous	
Cafe Cakes		Kids Party Food		Tapas, Antipasto & Mezze	
Cafe Food		Last-minute Meals		Tarts	
Casseroles		Lebanese Cooking		Tex-Mex	
Casseroles & Curries		Low-Fat Delicious		Thai Favourites	
Char-grills & Barbecues		Low Fat Fast		The Fast Egg	
Cheesecakes, Pavlova & Trifles		Malaysian Favourites		The Packed Lunch	
Chinese Favourites		Mince		Vegetarian	
Chocolate Cakes		Mince Favourites		Vegie Main Meals	
Christmas Cakes & Puddings		Muffins		Vietnamese Favourites	
Cocktails		Noodles		Wok	
Crumbles & Bakes		Noodles & Stir-fries		Young Chef	
Cupcakes & Cookies		Outdoor Eating			
Curries		Party Food			
Dried Fruit & Nuts		Pickles and Chutneys			
Drinks		Pasta		TOTAL COST £	

Photocopy and complete coupon below

Name _____

Address _____

_____ Postcode _____

Country _____ Phone (business hours) _____

Email*(optional) _____
* By including your email address, you consent to receipt of any email regarding this magazine, and other emails which inform you of ACP's other publications, products, services and events, and to promote third party goods and services you may be interested in.

I enclose my cheque/money order for £ _____ or please charge £ _____
to my: ☐ Access ☐ Mastercard ☐ Visa ☐ Diners Club

Card number | | | | | | | | | | | | | | | |

3 digit security code *(found on reverse of card)* _____

Cardholder's
signature _____ Expiry date ____ /____

To order: Mail or fax – photocopy or complete the order form above, and send your credit card details or cheque payable to: Australian Consolidated Press (UK), 10 Scirocco Close, Moulton Park Office Village, Northampton NN3 6AP, phone (+44) (01) 604 642200, fax (+44) (01) 604 642300, e-mail books@acpuk.com or order online at www.acpuk.com
Non-UK residents: We accept the credit cards listed on the coupon, or cheques, drafts or International Money Orders payable in sterling and drawn on a UK bank. Credit card charges are at the exchange rate current at the time of payment.
All pricing current at time of going to press and subject to change/availability.
Postage and packing UK: Add £1.00 per order plus 75p per book.
Postage and packing overseas: Add £2.00 per order plus £1.50 per book. **Offer ends 31.12.2007**